I0720268

If You Only Knew

Other works by Dennis Sampson

The Double Genesis

Forgiveness

Constant Longing

Needlegrass

For my Father Falling Asleep at Saint Mary's Hospital

Within the Shadow of a Man

The Lunatic in the Trees

Selected Poems

What More Could the Universe Want

What It Must Be Like for You

If You Only Knew

Poems

Dennis Sampson

Homestead Lighthouse Press

Copyright © Dennis Sampson, 2026. All rights reserved. No part of this book may be reproduced or transmitted in any form without the prior written permission of the publisher.

Library of Congress Cataloging-in-Publication Data
Names: Sampson, Dennis, 1949-author.
Title: *If You Only Knew* / Dennis Sampson.
Description: 796 W. Market Stret, Apt. C
Akron, Ohio 44303

ISBN 978-1-950475-47-6

Homestead Lighthouse Press
796 W. Market Stret, Apt. C
Akron, Ohio 44303
www.homesteadlighthousepress.com

Distributed by Homestead Lighthouse Press, Amazon.com, Barnes & Noble, and other booksellers and distributors.

Homestead Lighthouse Press gratefully acknowledges the generous support of its readers and patrons.

Book cover and interior design by Ray Rhamey, Ashland, OR
The Sloth, a poem by Theodore Roethke

Table of Contents

The Sloth

In moving slow he has no Peer.
You ask him something in his Ear,
He thinks about it for a Year;

And, then, before he says a Word
There, upside down (unlike a Bird),
He will assume that you have Heard—

A most Ex-as-per-at-ing Lug.
But should you call his manner Smug,
He'll sigh and give his Branch a Hug;

Then off again to Sleep he goes,
Still swaying gently by his Toes,
And you just know he knows he knows.

If You Only Knew

Lorca would have looked outside if he
had heard that cry. Neruda too. I will never be
the poet they became by listening to the sounds
of the night. I lie still, for a long time,

I, who belong to no one, to solitude, to the single dream
of following a thought as far as possible
without going out of my mind.
You know this. You have heard this before.
You who are always serenely rising above it all.

Mortal Words

Death you are precious. A savior
of sorts. You work so hard,
withering the last of those dandelions
along the fence line that had asked

the yellow butterflies to dance. Not a second's rest.
And no use trying to get you to stop. You're
inexhaustible. There you go again, death,
ordering all of your subordinates

who just want to go on living
to get their act together – as good
a disciplinarian there is for life itself.

Meadow

Four days it had rained and I had convinced myself
how little I cared, how great our arrogance,
nothing left but laughter
for the bureaucrat at a long table finding just the right lie
for a missile hitting civilians in Gaza.
What was missing in my life but a look at the beautiful?

I didn't expect them. Golden horses this morning
glad to be where they were, in the middle of this April—
not so close along the fence they had to pay any attention
to one another, not so far away as to be lonely.

Their manes and long tails
whipped by the wind—a wind that gave them a ghostliness
in sunlight seen from my slowed car along Chickasaw Road
splayed separating clouds—
their curved backs warmed in the meadow.

Let someone else complicate the visible world
with language working in service to the self.
What do you care who I am? Do you want to know?
Nothing could be less interesting in my seventy-fifth year.

Coming Across My First Book in a Used Bookstore

Beautiful in its own way, frayed at the edges, dark blue,
binder cracked, with frightening handwriting of three kinds
in the margins that I read quickly, reject outright,
puzzle over, accept. The dog-eared
pages are few. I read those pages carefully,
as if I were listening to the Buddha mumbling under his breath

from the lotus position. It has heft, is reticent, even respectful
unopened later on the table. Opened, it begins again
to speak with a passion I envy,
the preoccupation with God and the love of childhood
for the most part expected. Closed, it goes back
to being the velvet music box my mother coveted, playing

the same tune over and over again. It could be what
haunts one through a long life
of dead ends, and to which one refers occasionally
seeking to illuminate some principle related to innocence.
The sweat that went into it has dried up on the forehead
of the apprentice who gave it words
as tangible at times as touching a cat.

I run my hand over the cover. Open it again
to a bat, an azalea tufted with snow—a child under my supervision.
I address it as if it were capable of answering
and wonder how I wrote with such clarity
of a "tulip beautiful in exile," a cellar that "holds its breath,"
this story that for over two decades passed through hands
the last of which just gave it back to myself.

Three Days Before Thanksgiving and Already "Joy to the World"

and "We Wish You a Merry Christmas" are being sung in the supermarket. I've saved up all my hatred so I can seethe in silence beside the asparagus. *It's not too late. You can be grateful. But you have got to learn to put your wrath aside.*

*

The clueless hillside tombstones in Forsyth cemetery ascend to the level of the tree tops of this city. I find them refreshing. Last night, sleepless, I lay once again thinking of my life as if I were watching a movie that kept getting better and better until right at the climactic moment I scarcely could endure what was about to begin. I was breathless.

"What do you think the chances are this life is an illusion and what we dream reality?" I ask Ann, a local therapist—my friend.

"50-50" she says, without expression.

*

After an argument with her twelve-year-old daughter that ends with Laura taking the dog out into the dark and hiding by the fence, Ann says, over the phone, "I walked right by her and she didn't even flinch."

*

I remember when my father was dying how much in awe I was that he
had weeks, maybe days before he would enter the inexplicable mystery.
I whispered: "Your brother Harlan is waiting—you can go on." But he
hung in there. Now, at the Veterans Cemetery in Minneapolis in win-
ter, I gaze out at all the white crosses and say to my youngest sister, "If
all these folks can die I guess we can too." For a minute dying does not
seem so impossible.

*

Alfred Kazan, commenting on the behavior of Randall Jarrell, "Bet-
ter to study the strangeness of the external world rather than to be
outraged by it."

*

This story I have for the world is beginning to take shape. It consists
of one man sitting alone underneath a flowering dogwood, doing two
things: watching very precisely what is going on around him from dawn
to dusk--even into evening—and remembering what his childhood was
like. The only problem is recalling enough of childhood to make a run
at this. So lie. Prevaricate.

Like the time Uncle Harlan faking as if to throw his car keys into the
lake and they slipped from his fingers. His wife Ruth was so furious she
wouldn't speak to him for a day, but he was half-drunk, happy. Next
morning he stripped and hunted underwater for a long time, but came
up with nothing. Now there is a metaphor for you. Key: meaning. Wa-
ter: subconscious. Man: in the dark.

*

Every now and then I'll glance at something, a chair, say, no one ever sits in, and it will take on a terrible pathos all its own. I am not going to go so far as to say this breaks my heart but there's something really awful about this. As a kid, staring out the kitchen window during rainstorms at laundry left on the clothesline, I experienced that same kind of sadness, those drenched tee-shirts and underwear and blue jeans and blouses... they seemed so bereft.

*

Once during ninth grade gym class the teacher asked us to take off our shoes so we wouldn't scuff the hardwood floor. I refused, because my socks had holes in them. I never wore those socks again, much as I had come to love them.

*

Dream last night where somebody spoke the word "abysmal" in regards to a conversation they had with one of my friends, a word I have never ever used in my life. What was it doing showing up in one of my dreams?

*

The Weather Channel flashes a question: "How fast can a turkey run?" It offers three answers: a) 15 mph b) 25 mph c) 35 mph." I don't wait for the answer but think of it later and wish I had. The image of a turkey running 35 mph hour through a stubble field chased by a man with a 30.6. Run turkey! Run!

*

Do the dead ever laugh? Or do they just respond to everything with
a wistful sadness? Yesterday at the lake I heard the geese planing in.
First they cleared the high trees, eight of them, and descended right
above my head, making a magnificent ruckus. Legs out, they skidded
over the surface and were still. I watched them drift, every now and
then dipping their beaks. Then they climbed up onto the bank where
I observed them fall sleep, standing on one leg, their black and white
faces buried underneath their wings.

*

The boy I was will never come again—such is the mercilessness of his-
tory. He seems neither to be waiting back there in the past, nor par-
ticularly interested in the future. No, that boy is oblivious. I leave him
there with the other irretrievables, even if I can't help looking back at
him while he examines a viceroy butterfly he has discovered floundering
in the dust, and that he picks up then places in his other hand. These
details contribute to my belief we are here at the very least to see and,
in seeing, suffer the elimination of first this illusion, then that. That is
what gratitude is to me.

Wind shakes things up, overturning the chair in the yard, hurling the
aluminum bowl across the porch. It rattles the windows, searches all
the pockets of the evergreens, then runs away and conceals itself. The
cheap bird feeder sways, as if at a seance, and the clouds are driven
like a caravan of nomads across the heavens. The wind: it is having
such fun. At night it bangs, howls, breaks into the shed and, finding
nothing there, goes to sleep underneath the tarpaulin covering my
neighbor's outboard motor, passed out, perfectly content.

*

The honey in its pulp, the final found, the modest accomplishment, the abundance of the year and of the world.

My Rivers

The Seine that I will never be able to pronounce.
Same goes for Seurat, the pointillist. And the river Ouse
dreaming as I dream eternally
of carrying the corpse of Virginia Woolf unsuccessfully

out to sea. And the Volga too where, during the siege of Stalingrad
even the horror was frozen solid.
Twain's Mississippi running through his heart.

What was the name of the river that, for Siddhartha,
contained all that there was and is?
Dante's Tiber, Dante's Styx.

A mixture of blood and excrement
flowing forward as all rivers do.

Heraclitus's river that he could not keep up with
because he could not maintain
so slow a pace.
The river Eliot refers to, as the river within us.

River.
River.

When a river of any kind begins to become representative
you should know that your life is
about ready to begin.

Thirst of the giraffe.
Legs spread wide along the Okavango.

The hippo prancing effeminately underwater
like a ballerina!
That's where Janet surrendered her dreadful life

and love of her sister to my Missouri,

her Nike tennis shoes one next to the other on the shoreline
in winter.
And Lethe – What about Lethe? – And the Far East that is always
far from me

where the mollycoddled little deity saw a corpse
slid into the brown water of the Ganges
and who then realized all was a lie.

What a river might have to say about a conversion,
the face of one dipped down then up.

River of sorrow, river of joy.
The river that has everything and nothing to do with us
in any way whatsoever.

A Maple Leaf Come to Rest Underneath a Coffin
in Early October in a Small Town in Kentucky

He was the new priest presiding over the burial
of a young blonde receptionist the same age as his late wife,
a papist, as someone had shouted out to him
hurrying his bottle of Jack Daniels back to the Motel 6
one night from a mandatory conference for ministers in Kentucky.
Before the casket wrapped in elaborate scaffolding was lowered
he caught sight of a maple leaf curled underneath
her brass coffin that he could not take his eyes off. Then,
after everything had been said, the inconsolable husband
in a gesture of what seemed like defiance
seized the bewildered priest as if to prevent him from falling
from where he lingered in his odd mind
to a darker constituency.

God

cobweb drifting, psychotic house fly on the window sill,
spotted moth
fluttering down under my collar, to my annoyance,
the oncologist who wants you to know.
Starlings massing. And the bringing out of stars
and what there is to wonder about
with images more important than what the image implies.
What you loved and has survived
in the middle of the night, in the middle of your life,
cobweb pirouetting now, a child teething, fright,
consciousness so few know about,
the nearness of pontificating flowers, all anonymous,
hangman's knot,
the precious breath of a beloved dog into my nostrils,
that sorority girl in flip-flops
stopped on the interstate hurrying a turtle across the tarmac,

God no matter what

along with seeing that can't be realized in one lifetime –
that sunset-colored lady slipper's orchid spiraling,
bronze flow of clouds
over Little Rock, Arkansas, twilight, autumn, windless,
Cassiopeia's loyalty.
Life licked and delivered. Of nothingness derived.
That nut-hatch eating upside down in springtime,
the swearing in, the betrayal,

the syringe, the x-ray, the night nurse in a hurry to get
to her Dodge Dart.
*In the beginning god created the heavens and the earth
and the earth was void, and without form.*

Ceremonies

When the anonymous chest cavity of a cadaver
is cracked open, an exhalation of steam
is released – as beautiful as a bride of snow, brief
          as a spray of sea water. Listen. You can
hear the heart of the nineteenth century
author of *Adonis* being put away
to slosh in solitude in a jar of formaldehyde

and you can go to Hell
where Eurydice combs her wild white hair
surrendering to one of her reveries,
and Paolo suffers the imminent orgasm,
positioning and re-positioning himself

in wind through the gloom. Elsewhere
my ex-wife Colleen lets fall her silk nightgown
after lifting it over her shoulders, arms up, shakes out
her light-brown locks, talking to herself
before getting up under the covers.

And the dead are listening to everything being said
craning their skeleton necks that creak.

And I am aware of great spaces
as I speak to this page that wants
to be spoken to – what's outer, what's inner,
that first heave of starlight

yielding up mitochondria, paramecium, DNA,
as my new neighbor from across Ryan Drive
sweeps headlights of his Lexus into his driveway,
steps out to scrutinize his huge two-story brownstone
for one mysterious instant before pissing
into the winter honeysuckle I watched his daughter trimming
day before last.

*

Nebulae. Black holes.
Frightening spiral galaxies twisting like lace scarves
drawn over the sofa
that one black ant scaled, exploring translucent folds,
raising its head as if it had caught the scent.

Nuthatch, lawn chair, stapler, pin curler, barrette,
wine glass, disposable camera – the silverback gorilla grieving
while bearing its dead infant around and around on its back
in a photograph on the wall above my desk
– coin, carapace, ash tray, statue, skull and headstone.
Liz's shimmering red satin dress. My underpants.
My Yankees baseball hat. My mints.

        The dead have what they want
and then some,

        poring through golden file folders
as if an automatic rifle were trained on them –
cistern, poinsettia, silver letter opener, ballpoint pen, pin,
eighteen carat diamond on the finger of elderly Diane,
nave, violin, crucifix and crutch, crane and cauldron. Taser.

O death.

*

Down goes the deceased maple that stood so statuesquely
in the meadow, its shadows stretched like the tentative
cravings in the annunciation.

One man climbs
high within barren branches swinging his chain saw lithely,
slips, regains his balance. The thud of a lopped off branch
smacks the earth –

as final as any moral assessment –
and it is as if the lover and the loved had come face to face
in Elysium. And were nonplussed. "Name me
three birds that mate for life," I say to no one.
And no one answers back: "Cardinal, crow. And swan"
(which, of all the birds in the world, has a penis).

*

Scat, sarcophagus, blouse and shawl, bracelet
woven by the long elegant dark brown hands of the refugee
from Kenya, envelope (no stamp) addressed
in slanting script to immobilized Lucia in Olympia,

shovel, ax, the fork I always prefer (tough tines), sock
for which there is no match, used now to polish
my brown loafers. Tree decapitated, dismantled.
The fragrance of cut wood lingers in the air.

*

The meadow is a mess, the affluence of late summer
lost to the downright stinginess
of winter, stiff upright stems Liz gathered in my absence
at Thanksgiving, herself a mess,
with flashing black eyes that frightened me – stems arranged
and rearranged in a glass vase on the table
so their ascetic disposition might draw me nearer

when I pass them.

Shocking
the contribution a single candle confers
on a darkened dining room, phantoms of dead wildflowers
writhing on wall paper, the smell of sandalwood.
              And then the very first Christmas tree
glitters within the living room in the second brownstone on the left
on Balsam Avenue this last evening in November.

Father dead. Mother too. Better to concentrate exclusively
on the pleasantries of childhood than to consider
the brevity of everything: day-lily, day moon, night blooming cereus,

                    myself in swirling snow staring
into our lighted house at night from the yard when I was ten.

*

IED, machete, leather whip,
pincers, bastinado, lamp-shade created out of human skin,
judas cradle, cluster bomb,
thumbscrews, stocks, currycomb, Sobibor, saw, feigned grin of sympathy,
Theresienstadt, the propriety of every inquisition,
those precious little accoutrements adjusted in the casket
of the elderly Egyptian pharaoh traveling this life to the next.

*

One night, from under the covers in my plaid pajamas,
I got up, tip-toeing,
both sisters long asleep, Linda, lying face down,
Karen with her bare leg
dangling over the side like that of a castaway, mouth open. And I looked
first through the second story window to Adam's street to see

        if the bonfire was still burning, which it was, faintly,
then crept down the stairs, opening the screen door quietly.
Quietly closing it, into the cool night air. There

        where the cut branches of the dead elm tree
had snapped and sizzled in the afternoon, where the great
upward tongues of flame
wavered and drove us back, our hands held out before

        our faces, now only an otherworldly evanescence
pulsing and flickering. What was I doing there

in this night of all nights with autumn falling away into a past
I would come to call my own? The ash
was white, soft as snow. A tree limb crumbled then

                    and the bonfire remembered
it wasn't done devouring the old Dutch elm I had hustled up
only a week before, hollering my victory down,
no one to watch as I turned
toward the house, stepping lightly on bare soles, with the hush

                              and crackle dying:
only the spirit of that night left behind, at the center
of which a fire
flapped and writhed. And sleep came suddenly to me.

*

That inebriated green house fly is having difficulty
making up for the mistake of waking
to this warmth in February. It staggers
across the sill. Stops. It seems to plead. Revived, it whispers
up the filthy window pane, giving its whole insignificant
soul to this endeavor--a subtle hum in the ear.

Where did everybody vanish? this house fly
dragging its glittering
thorax into the sunlight seems to exclaim. Then, it is still.
It is lingering between one conviction and another.
This fly with its multifaceted eyes, copulating
for minutes after caressing like a blind man with its forelegs

the loved one's face (she extends her genitalia to him)
with ten hearts, 4,000 six-sided purplish lenses –
quintessence of ingenuity.

Mid-winter. Temperatures to be below
freezing tonight according to the paper. Winds gusting
robustly. A cold front bringing first light snow
from Knoxville to northern North Carolina. Then rain. Then sleet.

*

Even the priest needs to kick up his heels,
dance, run out under the stars with a bottle of Old Grandad,
shout up at the sky. Father Hopkins, don't be sorrowful.
Father Merton, swing with the deacons,
pirouette – do a back-flip. And you, my brother,
so downcast, won't you one more time
perform the hoochie coochie down the aisle for us?

Sing out of tune. Sing solo. Don't be shy,
your long slow voice floating up through the choir.
And the bigot will lie down with the adulteress,
the lion with the lamb, the orthodontist in drag,
the certified public accountant passed out under the stars.
You do not need a reason to praise the day,
this perfect night – this full moon over Birmingham.

*

Foreplay. Orgasm. Boredom. My father blowing his nose
looking out over the patio,
the poignant lifting of my mother's antique hand

open on his other shoulder. That lime green chameleon genuflecting.
And the femininity of the cheetah
in pursuit of the expressionless gazelle on the scorched savannah.

Piety. Cardiac arrest. Infanticide. Esophageal cancer. The
archbishop flatulent, a little hard of hearing. Crocuses opening all
at the same time all over Winston-Salem –
as if the secret of *dasein* had been passed around to them! Collusion.

Costume parties. Receptions. The apoplectic vocabulary
of crows. Repartee of beetles. Funerals. The soon-to-be sickening
look on the saint screaming "More fire!"
from her stake. And the wren officiating the ceremony
that begins, ends – that's all – the ceremonies of everyone everywhere.

Siddhartha Comes Incognito to North Carolina

In the calm of the night, in the quiet, the lights switched off in all the bedrooms,
the black lab that barked turned inward now, no cars,
a windless night too, the quarter moon evanescent in a corner of the sky,
bull bats veering, and the silhouette of a doe looking up a long time
as if it were representative of a thought that widens like ripples on an inlet
after a stone has been dropped, lifting the nauseating green scum

that finds another memory that proceeds in that light for the longest time
of the quarter moon until it shines, is gone,
for once, in a moment of time.
In the prolonged calm of this night. In the forbidden silence
with the river that moves—the river of remembrance—
moving as all rivers move through everything there is.

Sinister Possibilities

It is pointless to protest. And so I suffer
within the shadow of an ash
that tightens around me like a tourniquet.
Within this shadow also late in the morning

a thin lascivious strip of cerulean leather
stretches out on the black road, eyes open.
My dog senses this snake's sinister possibilities
and sniffs at the pulsing of its pale green throat.

Then this exquisite little whip whose heart's not in it,
tired of satisfying the vanities
of human wishes, with sunlight glimmering here,
there, disappears into the thick undergrowth,

an imperceptible tributary
of the great river that runs through the heart,
turns back, is purposeful.
And connects the contemptible to the blessed.

Whatever This Hour Might Be Called

In this dispassionate canticle providence belongs to the heron
concealing itself by staying still
on the cracked branch of driftwood on the other side
of the pond, and to the baby moccasin
rippling in the warmest water yellow there in sunlight

by the shore: belongs to summer thinning out the leaves,
the chickadee that uses its feet to break open
a sunflower seed, and the cardinal called Ecclesiastes
that does so by simply biting down –
to that woman with her black hair up at the supermarket

showing her milkwhite neck before the shampoos. It is evening.
Twilight. It is dusk. Where
within this burgeoning universe of supernovas and black holes
are you? – and what are we to conclude
of that lone crow flying low over the field with a saltine

in its mouth? It goes against the sorrows of the heart
to notice the reflection of the chicken hawk on noon water,
those blackbird's slanting shadows
across the sunlit bamboo outside the curtainless window
this morning. To see what is indisputable

while acknowledging that consciousness is...is what?
Providence belongs to the squallering too,
of the wren upset over having been
panicked from its nest in the dead fern hung from the front porch,
just as it does to the repercussions of the thunderstorm

blowing open both doors in a moment of delirium.
And that old banty rooster two condominiums down calls out *I Am*
this hour of night, whatever this hour might be called –
twilight? Evening? Dusk? –
and "What should I conclude from all this darkness?"

– as if he were the final philosopher on the corrugated lectern
of his hen house, fulfilling his obligation to a specific
line of thought: Cartesian, with a hint of Immanuel Kant,
Kierkegaard wringing his hands in Denmark.
The blue heron suddenly seen in all its godless solitude.

I Have Prepared Myself for the Void

one line from Lorca and the love
of a little sunlight on an old brick wall
that discovers a line of ants
in single file passing another line of ants
that asks What have you found?
They touch quickly and go forward.

All asking is over. The curved rind of the orange
issues its aroma long after you have vanished
like a shadow that thought it would be shadow
much longer, lengthening
then withdrawing – like one with second thoughts –

then lengthening again just before dusk. The void
is not what I thought it was. Is less.
Is more. A score by Brahms, a scared disciple,
a siren that ceases to be called
by one who is chained – who no longer cries out.

The Comedy in the Window

You have served your purpose, Alighieri.
You helped me get through two marriages and the death
that knocked me back. In Greensboro each April
I stare down at the grave of Randall Jarrell
and wonder what you did with that beautiful man.

Propped up in the window of my study
to keep out the setting sun
(which makes it difficult to see when I am scribbling)
who would have thought
you would have ended up blocking out the light
blinding you when you beheld Beatrice,
who was just doing what God wants?

Despite the twisted descriptions
in your *Comedy*, you inspire me
to write about finding you this afternoon
beside puny little Siddhartha,
adjusting you upside down,
in profile, with a blazing halo.
Frayed. Coming apart.

I hope you got what you wanted,
Beatrice naked to the waist.
"Go slow and kiss me with
an open mouth as long as He's
not watching." You have an eternity
to ravish her. To hell with the rest of us.

Cardinal and Wren

I'm not only that cardinal
I'm that wren,

the former operatic
while the latter screeches way back
in the evergreens unrelentingly

then shows up to look me in the face, outraged.
The little son of a bitch

with a feistiness that almost brings
me to my knees.

It's sweet to be both of these.

I'm listening to what it means to be bittersweet
while at the same time needing to put my foot down
in some meaningful way.

Maria Callas. Janis Joplin.
That prepossessing duality.
And so I accept myself as one as well as the other.

Mistaking Two for One

What was I searching for? Was I searching for anything?
Did I seek only to speak of what I'd seen sometimes in passing,
that god-like anonymous cedar that for years seemed just one cedar
until it was explained to me by Larry
one was two, cedars grown so close together, hands in hands,
my feelings were for both and all
that wind thrown through them one shared wind?

Sunlight splinters this January afternoon on isolated sleet
that's ghosted the lawn in shade, in covert corners. Over there
by the supplicating maple cardinals flock
to the feeders like splattered blood. They are courteous, accommodating.
One looks up. The other cocks its head and seems satisfied with this.

Curious to think they would behave as they do
even if I were not here. And yet how in the world
could they ever go on without me?

Getting Into Bed With The Odyssey

It suddenly dawned on me last night
reading in bed
that what I was being asked
when my father lay there his last hour
was to leave everything I had
and get up into that hospital bed with him
and vanish. I would lift my left leg
just so, slide up close,
burying my face in his back,
then take that death with me into
his bed sores, his stitches,
the ache in his upper neck
my ache, as well as his,
his bad breath my
bad breath. Some of us can actually correct
our mistakes
by letting ourselves be called back,
myself in memory
entering my father's death, my father's
private dialogue with who he was
and is, even as I questioned my right to ask him
if in his long life he was happy,
then slid *The Odyssey* back into its slot in the shelf.

That Laugh

That was my mother's laugh
I just laughed, a lilting not-too-loud laugh
when what she was thinking about struck her
as funny and I merely smiled at,

an anecdote remembered
that probably had something to do with her husband.
Why did I hear that laugh
just now

as if she were sitting in her blue chair
by the picture window,
a laugh as surely hers as it is mine now?
Old woman, welcome back

from the mute dead who are dreaming still
of what comes next,
returned to earth
that now means everything to them,

not as phantoms at the foot of a bed
but in that benevolent laugh
I just spoke of
after which something just clicked,

caught me off guard,
remembering how much a part
of my life yours still is.

THE END

www.ingramcontent.com/pod-product-compliance
Lightning Source LLC
Chambersburg PA
CBHW021746190726
48288CB00009B/3177